The Poo that Animals Do

... and Tony De Saulles

WAYLAND
www.waylandbooks.co.uk

Published in Great Britain in paperback in 2018 by Wayland

Copyright © Hodder & Stoughton, 2017

Editor: Melanie Palmer
Designers: Peter Scoulding and Cathryn Gilbert
Picture researcher: Diana Morris

ISBN: 978 1 5263 0395 0

An imprint of
Hachette Children's Group
Part of Hodder & Stoughton
Carmelite House
50 Victoria Embankment
London EC4Y 0DZ

An Hachette UK Company
www.hachette.co.uk
www.hachettechildrens.co.uk

Printed in China

The website addresses (URLs) included in this book were valid at the time of going to press. However, it is possible that contents or addresses may have changed since the publication of this book. No responsibility for any such changes can be accepted by either the author or the Publisher.

Picture credits: Ajay PTP/Shutterstock: 26t.alybaba/Shutterstock: 8t.Aaron Amat/Shutterstock: 21tr.By/Shutterstock: 21tl.Rafal Chicawa/Shutterstock: 26b.pan demin/Shutterstock: 6t.Celso Diniz/Shutterstock: 18t.Dmitry design/Shutterstock: 25b.Dennis W Donahue/Shutterstock: 27t. elbud/Shutterstock: 21b.emka74/ Shutterstock: 4bc, 16tl, 32tc. Steve Estvanik/Shutterstock: 27c.Everett Historical/Shutterstock: 29bl.Jozsef Szasz-Fabian/Shutterstock: 4br, 7tl, 32tr.FLPA/FLPA: 10.Tyler Fox/Shutterstock: 25t.David Gallaher/ Shutterstock: 23b.Andrey Gudkov/Shutterstock: 11br. Horus2017/ Shutterstock: 4bl, 7tcr, 32tl.Eric Isselee/Shutterstock: 7b, 15b, 17b. Kokhanchikov/Shutterstock: 13b.A V Kost/Shutterstock: 19b.Sarin Kunthong/Shutterstock: 24t.Erik Lam/Shutterstock: 23t.leisuretime70/ Shutterstock: 4bcr, 32 tcr. James Martin: 4bcl, 7tr, 32tcl.W Scott McGill/Shutterstock: 28t.Milles Studio/Shutterstock: 9c.natchapohn/ Shutterstock: 15c.Erwin Niemand/Shutterstock: 20b.Natalia Paklina/ Shutterstock: 20tr.PK.Phuket studio/Shutterstock: 17c.Poozeum/ Wikimedia Commons: 29cl.Tinus Potgieter/Shutterstock: 13t.Michael Potter 11/Shutterstock: 12t.Dan Quinsey/Wikimedia Commons: 29cr.Rasika108/Shutterstock:27b.Romas_Photo/Shutterstock: 14b. Simon Shim/Shutterstock: 24br. sirtravelalot/Shutterstock: 18c.sitayi/Shutterstock: 22c.Yulia Sonsedska/Shutterstock: 16tr. Studiovin/Shutterstock: 4tr.Super Prin/Shutterstock: 11t. Andrew Sutton/Shutterstock: 14t.trubavin/Shutterstock: 9b.Vita Serendipity/ Shutterstock: 11bl.Wikimedia Commons: 29br.wildestanimal/ Shutterstock: 8b.Ton Witsarut/Shutterstock: 4bccl, 7tcl, 32tccl.Anke van Wyk/Shutterstock: 3b, 4tl, 16b. YoOnSpy/Shutterstock: 24bl.

Every attempt has been made to clear copyright. Should there be any inadvertent omission please apply to the publisher for rectification.

Contents

The POO detectives

Animal poos come in all different shapes, sizes, colours and smells. In fact, an expert poo detective can look at one and tell you which animal left it behind.

Maybe you'd like to try being a poo detective? Look at the images below and see if you can work out which animal produced them.

Guess whose poo?

These are the poos of a cow, dog, elephant, fish, mouse and rabbit. (You can check your answers on page 32.)

1   2   3   4   5   6

Time for some SCIENCE ...

The Poo Cycle

Ever trodden in a dog poo? If so you might think we would be better off without poo. But poo is actually an important part of the natural world.

This bear pooing in a wood shows why:

❶ Bear poos in the wood

POOP!

❷ Poo breaks down and becomes part of the soil

❸ Plants (such as huckleberries) grow in the soil

❹ Bear eats either plants (bears LOVE huckleberries!) or animals that have eaten the plants

❺ Bear digests food and ...

POOP!

World of poo

There's a whole world of animal poo out there. From the poo that could make you rich, to square poos, or the poo that produces the world's most expensive coffee. Read on to find out what's so great about animal poo!

5

Do jellyfish POO?

In other words, are jellyfish also smellyfish? The answer really depends on what you mean by 'poo'.

If by 'poo' you mean, 'dollop of something brownish and smelly', that is not really what jellyfish do. They just shovel food in, suck out what they need, and release a slimy gloop that goes out the same way it came in.

YUK!

SHPLOOP!

That *does* sound disgusting – but it doesn't sound like poo as we know it.

Complicated Poo

The stuff we recognise as poo comes from animals with bodies much more complicated than a jellyfish's. In this kind of animal, food passes through different parts of its body, and something different happens to the food at each stage. What finally emerges at the end of this process is poo.

MOUSE POO   COW POO   DOG POO   FISH POO

Although all poos are produced in a similar way, they look different depending on the animal's size and what it eats.

Time for some SCIENCE ...

What Makes Poo Poo?

Poo is the solid (or nearly solid) material that comes out when living creatures have finished digesting food.

This leopard eating a fish will show you how it works:

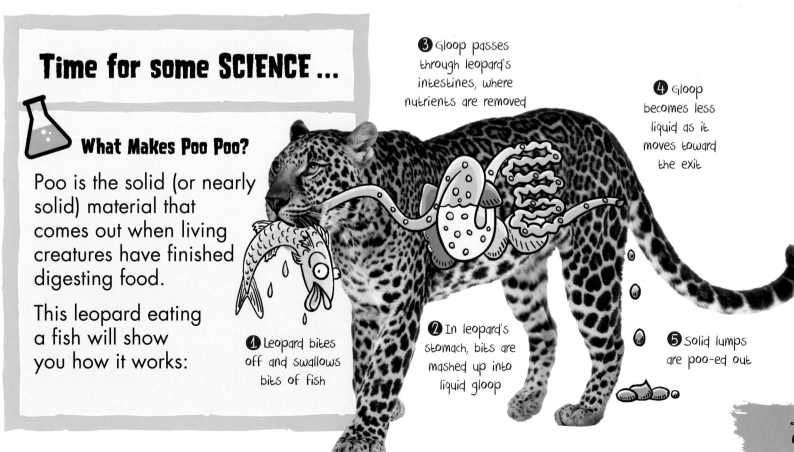

❶ Leopard bites off and swallows bits of fish

❷ In leopard's stomach, bits are mashed up into liquid gloop

❸ Gloop passes through leopard's intestines, where nutrients are removed

❹ Gloop becomes less liquid as it moves toward the exit

❺ Solid lumps are poo-ed out

Pricey POO!

Poo can be very valuable. Imagine finding one worth £40,000. That's what happened to eight-year-old Charlie Naysmith.

Charlie found a lump of ambergris on the beach in Dorset, UK in 2012. Ambergris is pooed out by sperm whales. It is often used to make expensive perfumes. Charlie's lump only weighed about 600 grams. Worth looking out for next time you're on a beach!

Poo from a sperm whale, known as ambergris

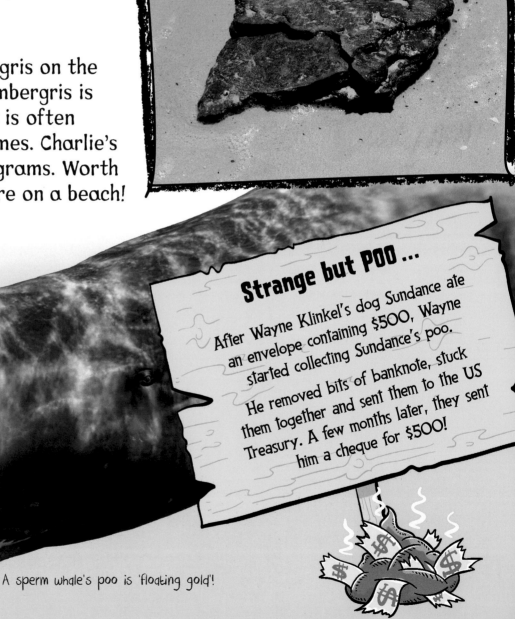

A sperm whale's poo is 'floating gold'!

Strange but POO ...

After Wayne Klinkel's dog Sundance ate an envelope containing $500, Wayne started collecting Sundance's poo.

He removed bits of banknote, stuck them together and sent them to the US Treasury. A few months later, they sent him a cheque for $500!

The bird-poo war

In the 1860s, Chile, Peru and Spain fought a war over poo. The war was about the Chincha Islands. The islands were rich in guano (another name for bird poo). Guano is a valuable fertiliser.

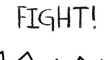

FIGHT!

Poo coffee

If anyone ever offers you a cup of kopi luwak, think twice. It is coffee made from beans that have been eaten – and then pooed out – by civets. Civets are about as big as a medium-sized dog with a face like a raccoon's. Apparently, being pooed out by a civet gives the coffee beans extra flavour.

Kopi Luwak coffee beans

Civets are related to the cat family

ONE LUMP OR TWO?

9

POO defences

Most of us find poo unpleasant. Because of this, some animals use poo as a defence system.

Pygmy sperm whale

NO ONE messes with a normal-sized sperm whale – but the smaller pygmy version sometimes gets attacked. So if it sees a predator coming, the little whale squirts out a big load of poo, then fans the water with its tail. This makes a poo cloud to hide inside.

IT'S A DIRTY TRICK, BUT IT WORKS!

PRRRP!

YURGH!

GET LOST!

SPLURP!

The hoopoe

If you get too close to a nest of hoopoe chicks, they hiss at you. Move away quick! If you don't, they squirt a jet of poo at your eyes.

The potato beetle

Imagine COVERING yourself in poo to avoid being eaten. That's what the baby potato beetle does. (At least it uses its own poo, not someone else's.) The beetle's poo is toxic, so it provides a double defence.

THE ONE WHO DUNG IT, FLUNG IT!

Strange but POO...

Gorillas warn off intruders by:

1. Roaring
2. Drumming their chest
3. Throwing poo*

* Number 3 is unpleasant but not as bad as number 4, which is being torn limb from limb!

11

The POO nursery

Dung beetles have a special bond with poo. They use it as a nursery for their young.

When they breed, they roll up a ball of animal poo, bury it, and lay their eggs inside. When the eggs hatch, the poo provides their young with something to eat. Yuk!

Months later, the young beetles dig their way to the surface and appear from the ground, as if by magic.

Dung beetles can roll a ball of poo that is up to 10 times their own weight

Beetle eggs hatch

Young beetles eat poo

Beetles dig to the surface

AH! FRESH AIR!

Around the world, the dung beetle's strange life has led to many myths about it:

In South Asia, people thought the world was first made when a dung beetle brought back a ball of earth from the bottom of the sea.

South America's Chaco people said a giant dung beetle made the first man and woman from clay.

Strange but POO...

Ancient Egyptians linked the dung beetle's poo-rolling habits to the sun rolling across the sky each day.

Inscriptions at Karnak Temple, Egypt

13

POO extremes

What kind of animal's poo is so big it could fill a swimming pool? Which animal does the stinkiest poo? Meet the extremes of the animal poo world:

Biggest

Blue whales eat up to 3.6 tonnes a day. They do the world's biggest poos: one poo could easily fill a swimming pool!

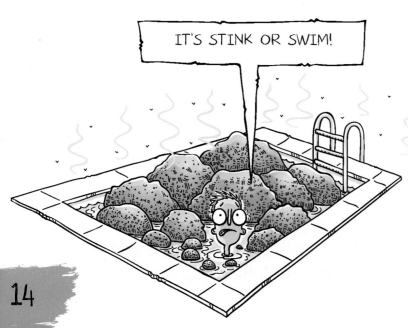

IT'S STINK OR SWIM!

Stinkiest

These come from orangutans that have been eating durian fruit (which already smells like poo even before being eaten).

Time for some SCIENCE ...

What makes blue whale poo orange?

A blue whale's orange poo colour comes from its main food, krill. Krill contain astaxanthin, a red chemical. The astaxanthin passes through the whale, and dyes its poo orange.

Least Often

The three-toed sloth climbs down from the trees to poo only once a week.

TUESDAY IS POOS DAY!

YIKES!

Highest

The skipper caterpillar can fire its poo up to 1.5 metres – that's like one of yours hitting the top of Nelson's Column!

15

Food from POO

Most of the goodness has been removed from poo by the time it is released. Sometimes, though, enough is left to provide a meal.

Eating your own poo

Animals as different as rabbits and elephants sometimes eat their own poo. When a rabbit poos out used food for the first time, it does it in its burrow and eats the poo. When that poo passes through and plops out a second time, the rabbit does it outside and leaves the poo there.

Oh yum! Even better SECOND time round.

WHAT'S FOR DINNER, MUM?

POOP OF THE DAY!

Eating other animals' poo

Some small creatures eat the poo of others. Rats and mice eat poo to find bits of undigested food. Many ants eat bird poo, and flies love to tuck in to all kinds of dung.

SLURP!

CHOMP!

GUZZLE!

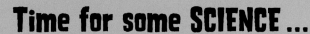

Time for some SCIENCE...

Poo Medicine

Some animals eat poo for medical reasons.

Baby rhinos, for example, eat the poo of adults to collect bacteria they need. (If you feel like telling a baby rhino that's disgusting... good luck!)

Once the bacteria have set up home, the poo eating can stop.

The POO travel service

Some of what animals eat does not get digested. Instead, it travels around inside the animal for a while. Then, usually a day or so later, it is released inside a poo.

Fruit seeds are often transported in this way. Once released, the seed begins to grow. Sometimes the seed even uses nutrients from the poo to get a head start.

Fruit-eating animals

① Macaw eats fruit

② Macaw poo contains fruit seeds

③ Seeds from poo grow in soil

④ Macaw eats fruit

Animals such as bears and parrots eat fruit. The poo travel service they provide helps plants spread across a wide area of land.

Time for some SCIENCE ...

Doggy Navigation

Scientists have suggested that dogs prefer to poo in a north-south direction. This may mean that dogs have an internal compass. Perhaps this explains how some dogs have navigated huge distances.

PRPP!

Strange but POO ...

The white sandy beaches of many desert islands are mostly made of parrotfish poo. The sand is created when parrotfish eat coral reefs. The bits of coral are broken up inside the fish, and come out as sand.

Animal TOILETS

Some animals poo wherever they feel like it. Others prefer to use a special toilet space. They do this for all sorts of reasons.

Lemurs like to poo together as a way of making friends.

Northern collared lemmings use underground toilets to avoid predators while having a poo.

meerkats, hyenas and **European badgers** all mark their territory using carefully placed toilets.

Social networking through poo

Some animals use toilets as a kind of social network. Their poo contains all sorts of messages for other animals to read. The poo reveals who left it behind, how long ago they were there, what they had been eating, or whether they were sick. It might even reveal whether they are looking for a mate. One animal that LOVES to catch up using a poo message board is the rhino. Rhinos often stamp about in poo piles, stirring up the latest news.

News at Pong ...

A SICK ELEPHANT WITH AN UPSET TUMMY WAS HERE THIS MORNING ...

TELL ME ABOUT IT, I JUST TROD IN IT!

Time for some SCIENCE ...

Messages In Poo

How can poo pass on messages? The answer is smell.

Dogs, for example, have an incredible sense of smell. If dogs had vision as good as their sense of smell, they would be able to see things 4,800 km away (compared to a human's 0.5 km). To a dog, a poo is FULL of pongy messages about who left it and how they were feeling.

SNIFF, SNIFF!

POO camouflage

Prey animals can often tell a predator is coming because they smell it. But if you're a predator, there's one very effective way to avoid detection ...

You roll in some strong-smelling poo.

SHPLURP!

Poo: the perfect outfit

Rolling in poo disguises the predator's smell by covering it with another animal's. Wolves, jackals and lions all roll in the poo of their prey animals whenever they get the chance.

HA, HA, HA, HE, HE, HE, MY BUNNY DINNER CAN'T SMELL ME!

Pet dogs probably roll in strong-smelling poo for the same reason. All dogs are descended from wolves. They are pre-programmed to dive in, whenever a poo roll is possible.

Why Does Poo Smell (Bad)?

It's because of bacteria. Bacteria live in an animal's intestines. As food passes through, the bacteria break it down.

Sometimes, the bacteria produce a chemical called sulphur. It is sulphur that gives poo its special smell.

Not all poo smells bad, though. Some people say that elephant poo, for example, smells quite nice.

FREE CAMOUFLAGE

23

POO disguises

Some animals have evolved to look a lot like a poo. This is a great way of stopping yourself being eaten. After all, not many predators see a poo and think, 'Yum – lunch!'

Dung Spiders

Looking like a poo is a popular disguise among spiders. One of the best-known poo imitators is pasilobus, otherwise known as a bird dung spider. When it's all curled up, pasilobus does look very like the shiny, dark-coloured middle bit of a bird poo.

Close up of bird dung

A white spider imitates bird poo

Close up of a Bird Dung Crab Spider

YURK!

IT WASN'T ME!

Viceroy caterpillars

Being a caterpillar is a hard life. All sorts of animals want to eat you – birds in particular. The viceroy caterpillar has evolved a good way to avoid becoming bird lunch: it is disguised to look like a bird poo.

The swallowtail caterpillar mimics bird poo

I'D HAVE BEEN CROSSING MY LEGS FOR HOURS... IF I HAD LEGS!

Strange but POO...

Snakes are clean animals, and pet ones don't like to poo in their living space. Some owners claim to have toilet-trained their snake. They take it outside for a poo, then the snake comes back in when it's finished.

Human uses for animal POO

It is not only other animals that find animal poo useful. For centuries, humans have been finding all sorts of things to do with it.

Staying warm

Some kinds of animal dung can be burned on a fire after being dried out. This is especially useful in places where few trees grow. Dried yak poo, for example, is popular in the Himalaya mountains.

WE'VE DUNG WELL!

THERE'S MOUNTAINS OF IT!

Cow dung laid out to dry in Varansi, India

Building with poo

In Europe in the Middle Ages, cow dung was sometimes used as a building material. Some of the buildings made with it are still standing. In Africa and Asia, dung is still used in the walls and floors of some buildings.

Cow dung being dried and used to make walls

OOOOOOH, IT'S LOVELY AND WARM ...

Several animals use poo to build their homes. In Africa, the secretary bird loves to use a bit of zebra dung.

Strange but POO ...

In France, skidding in a dog poo with your left foot is said to bring good luck. A right-foot skid is bad luck, though.

In other places, being pooed on by a bird signals good luck.

27

Petrified POO

'Petrified' means turned to stone, or fossilised. Fossilised poo from millions of years ago can tell us a lot about the past.

Dinosaur poo

Fossilised dinosaur poo is called coprolite. By analysing coprolite, scientists can work out what particular dinosaurs used to eat. For example:

What's for tea, T-rex?

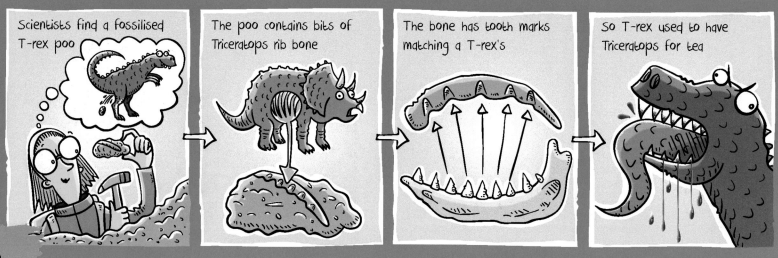

Scientists find a fossilised T-rex poo

The poo contains bits of Triceratops rib bone

The bone has tooth marks matching a T-rex's

So T-rex used to have Triceratops for tea

Strange but POO...

We are used to thinking of fossils as rare items. But coprolite is so common that there was once a coprolite mining industry in England.

Coprolite can be used to make phosphate, which is used in ammunition. During the First World War, Britain found it hard to get enough phosphate from the usual sources – so it started digging up coprolites instead.

Fossilised dinosaur poo

Soldiers with ammunition in the First World War

Coprolite miners in the 1880s

29

Animal poo: fast facts

Most frequent poo-ers: Rabbits produce about 500 poos per day (that's 20 an hour!) and geese poo roughly every 10 minutes.

Yukiest: The vulture poos on its own feet to kill off harmful bacteria.

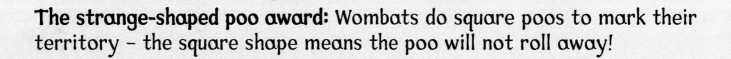

The strange-shaped poo award: Wombats do square poos to mark their territory – the square shape means the poo will not roll away!

The biggest poo-er on land: Elephants can produce about 50 kg a day.

Least frequent poo-er: Bears. When they hibernate, a plug of poo and hair forms. This stops any poo from popping out until the bear wakes up in spring.

Glossary

ammunition bullets and shells for use in guns

bacteria tiny living creature made up of just one cell

compass device that shows direction of north, south, east and west

digest turn food into substances the body can use

evolved developed and adapted over a long period of time

fertiliser product that helps plants grow faster and bigger

fossilised preserved from the past in rock or stone

guano type of bird poo; guano contains the chemicals nitrogen, phosphate and potassium, which plants need for growth

intestine bit of an animal's insides that connects their stomach with their bottom

krill small sea creature a bit like a shrimp

nursery place where the young are looked after

nutrient something in food that a living creature can use to stay alive or grow

predator animal that hunts and kills others

prey animal that is hunted by another as food

seed part of a plant from which a new plant grows

toilet train train an animal to poo and wee outside

toxic harmful substance

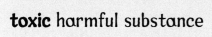

Answers (for page 4)

1	2	3	4	5	6
dog	fish	cow	rabbit	elephant	mouse

Find out more about poo

Animal Science: Poo, A Natural History of the Unmentionable (Walker Books, 2004)

Get the Scoop on Animal Poop! (Imagine! 2012)

Plop Trumps and Plop Trumps Extreme (a card game by Cheatwell Games, 2013)

The National Poo Museum, Isle of Wight runs exhibitions at Sandown Zoo and other locations around the country. Go to: www.poomuseum.org for more information.

The Museo della Merda, Castelbosco, Italy is all about cow poo. The museum is based around a project that uses cow poo to make electricity. Even the museum building is kept warm using heat generated from cow poo. See: www.museodellamerda.org

Index